Welcome to the underwater kingdom!
Here begins your oceanic adventure. Before you start remember your creativity is not limited to the illustrations, use the space around them to harness your imagination and create doodles of your own. Feel free to use the first page as practice! Good luck, once inside you may wish never to return!

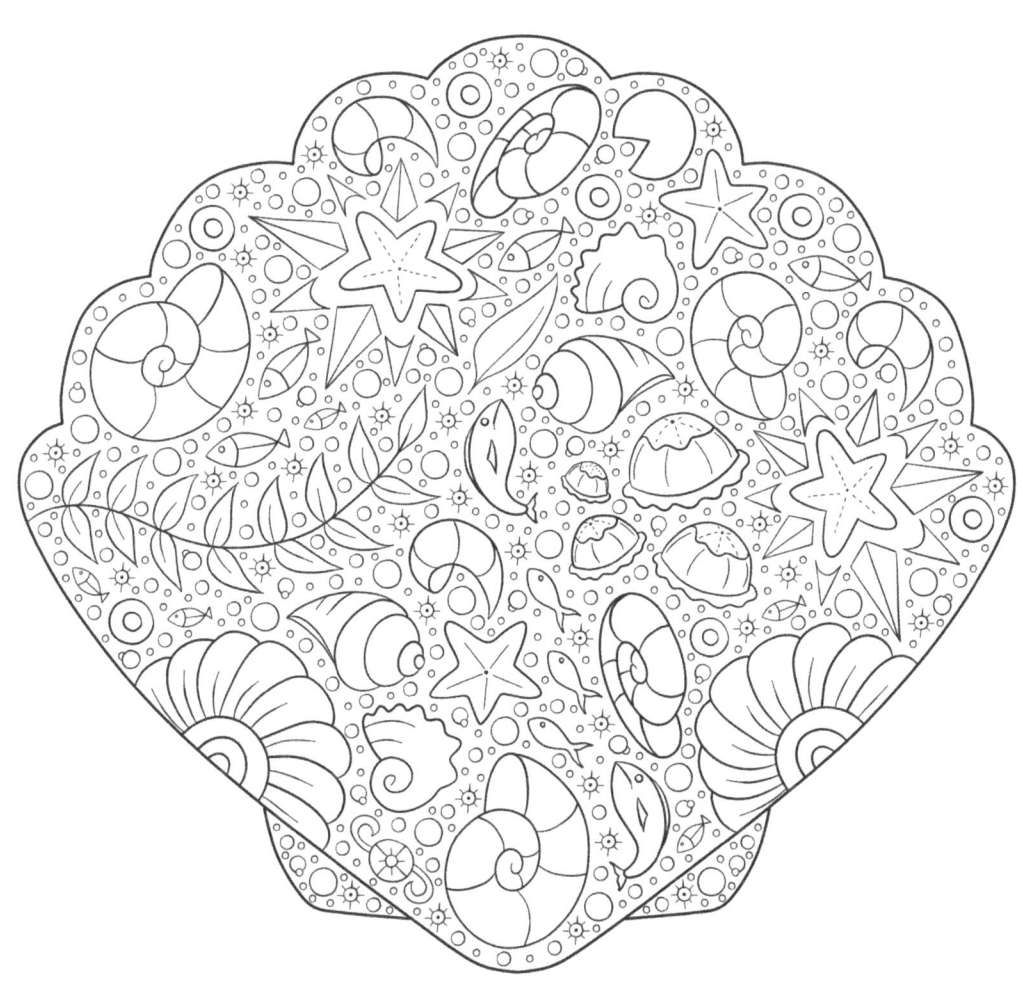

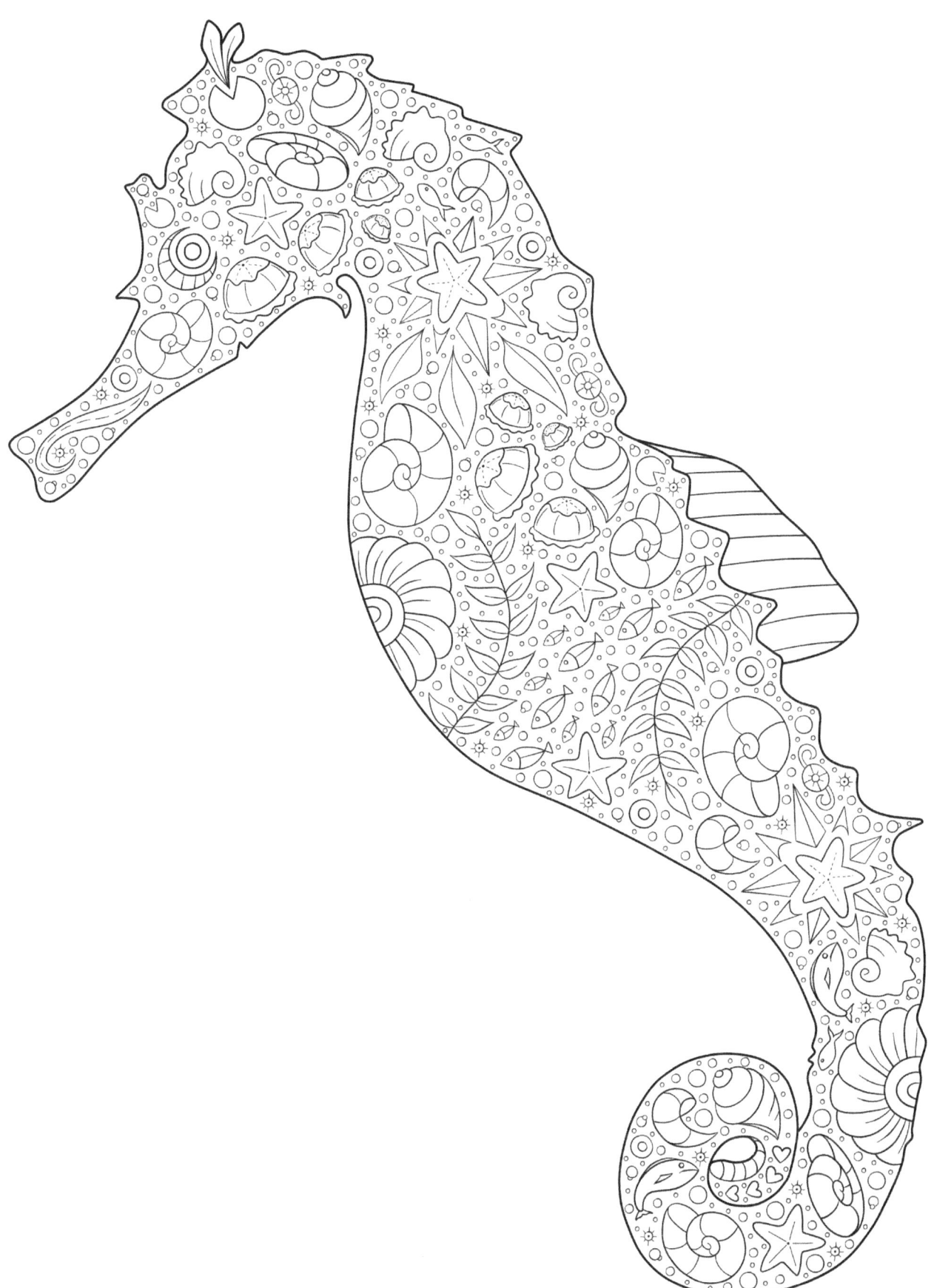

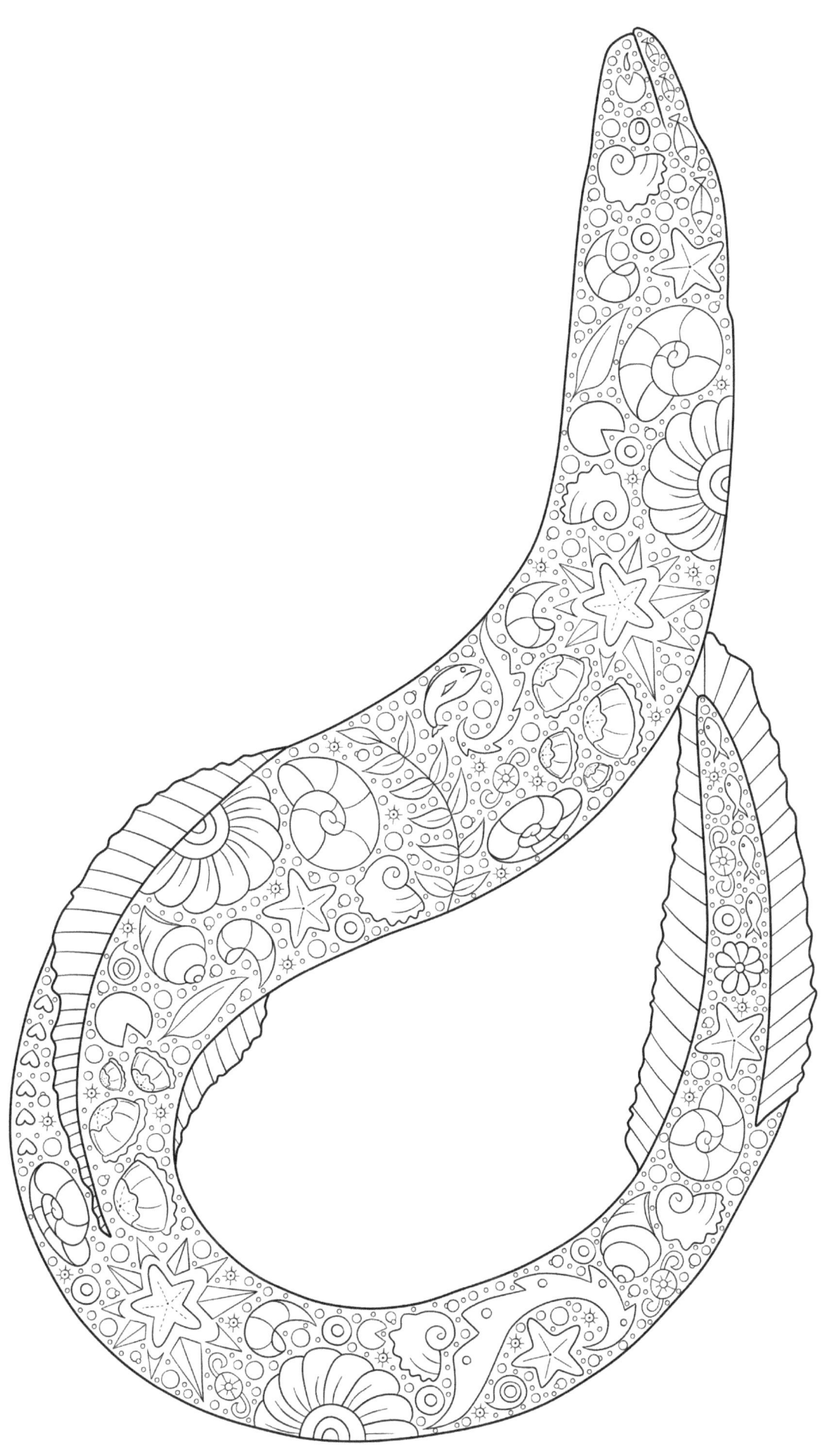

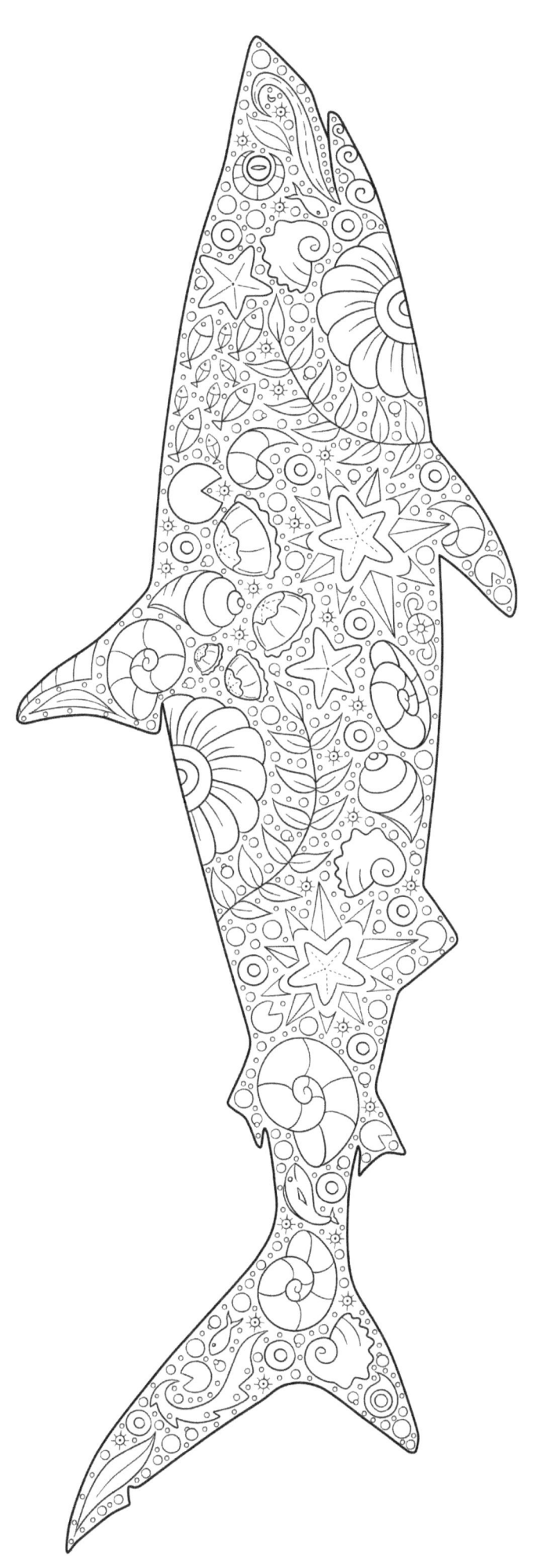

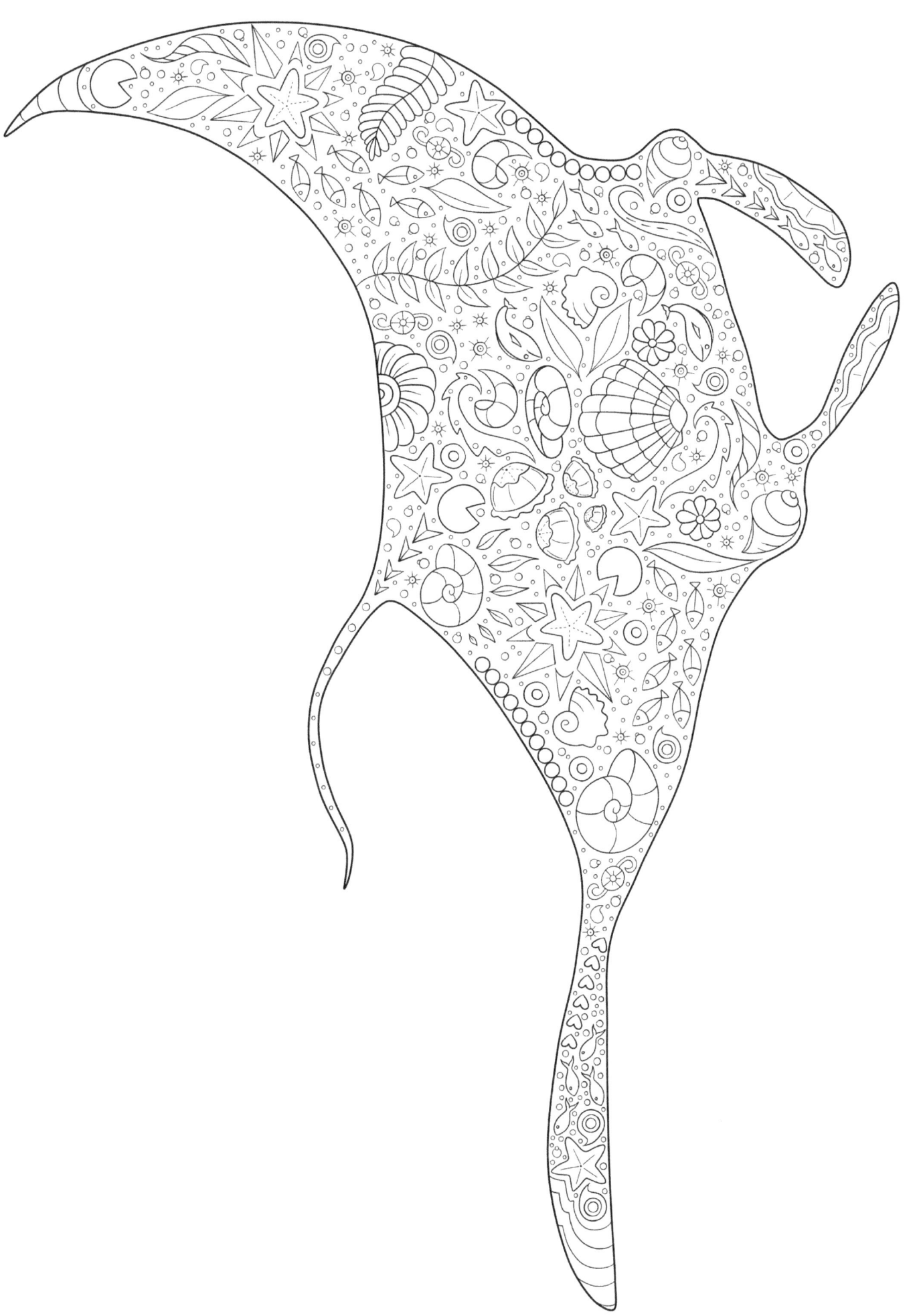

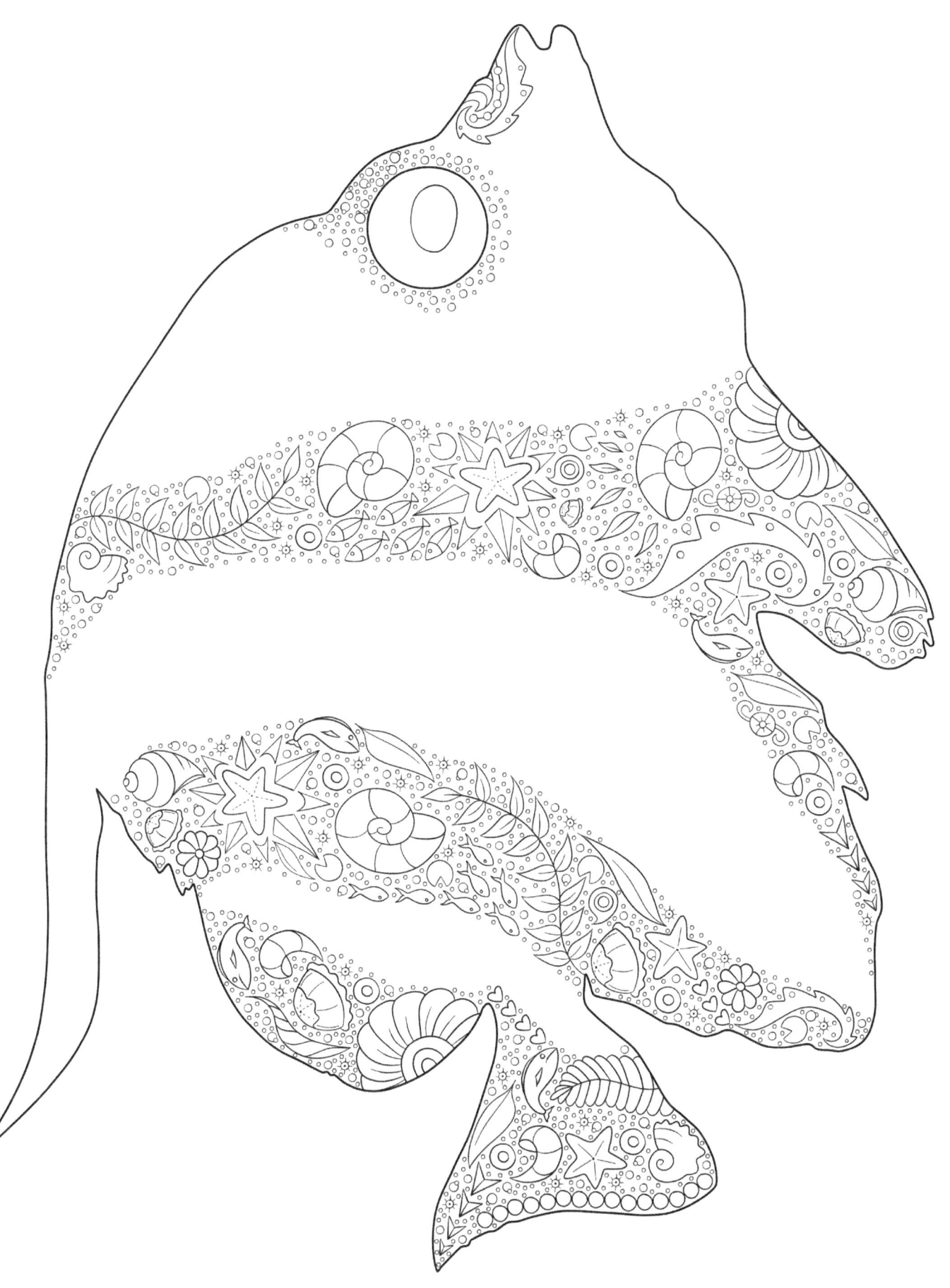

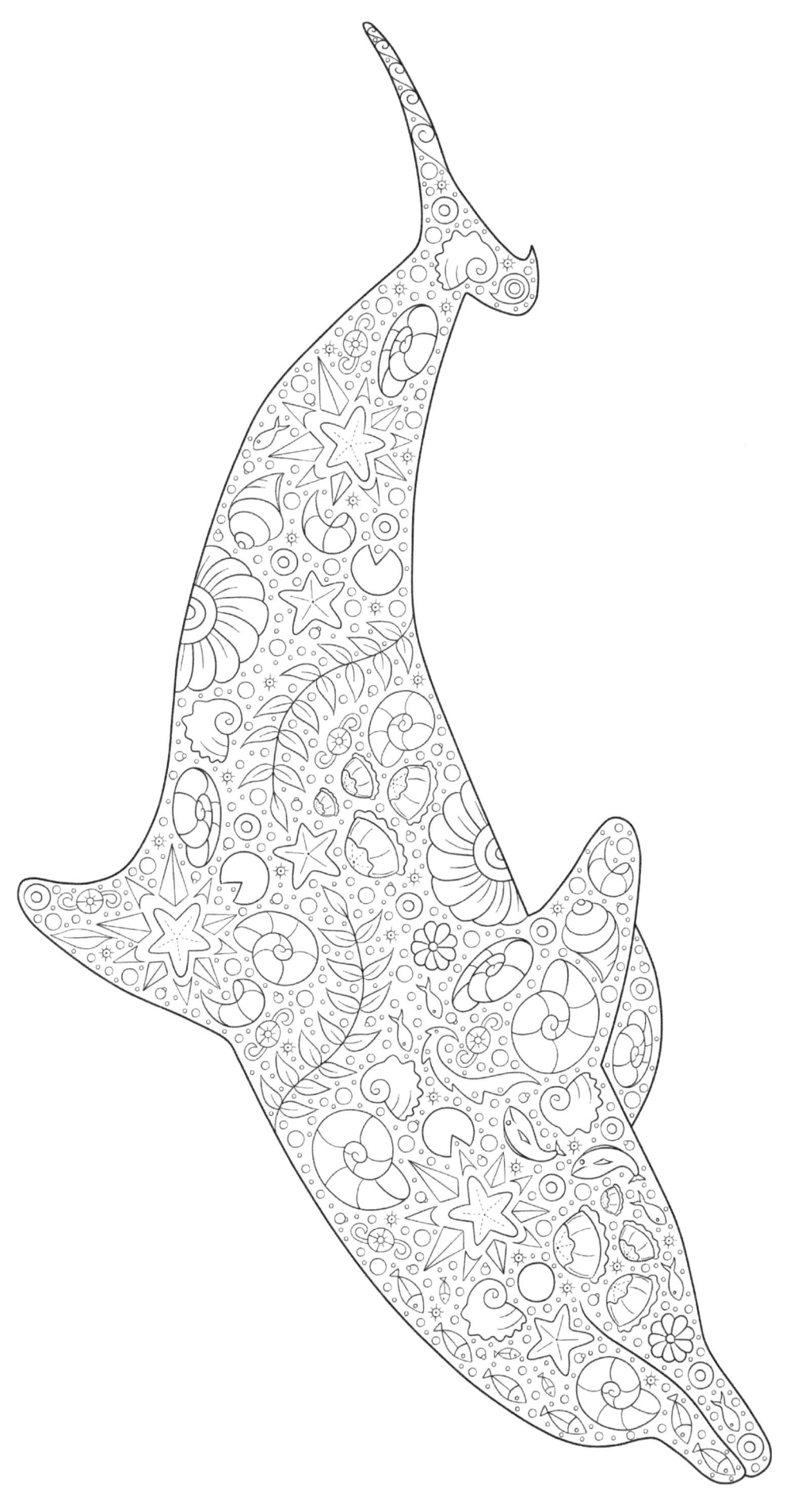

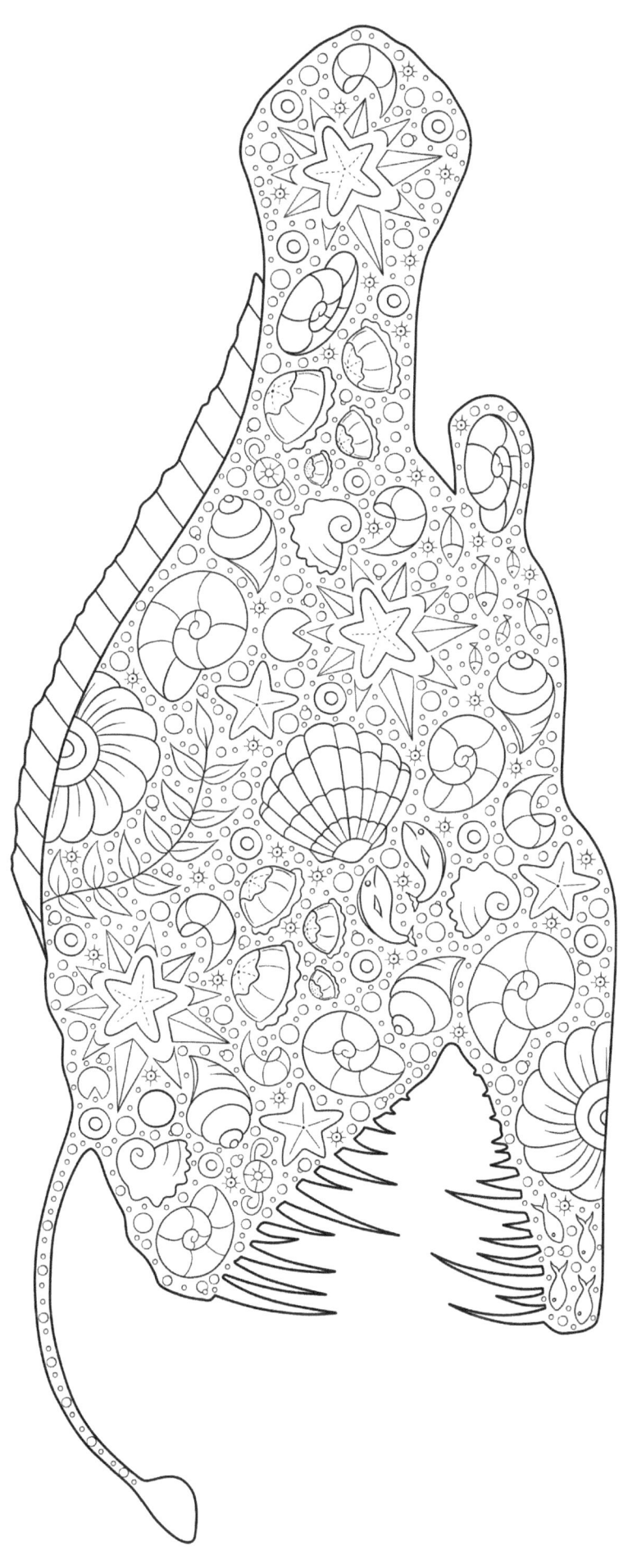

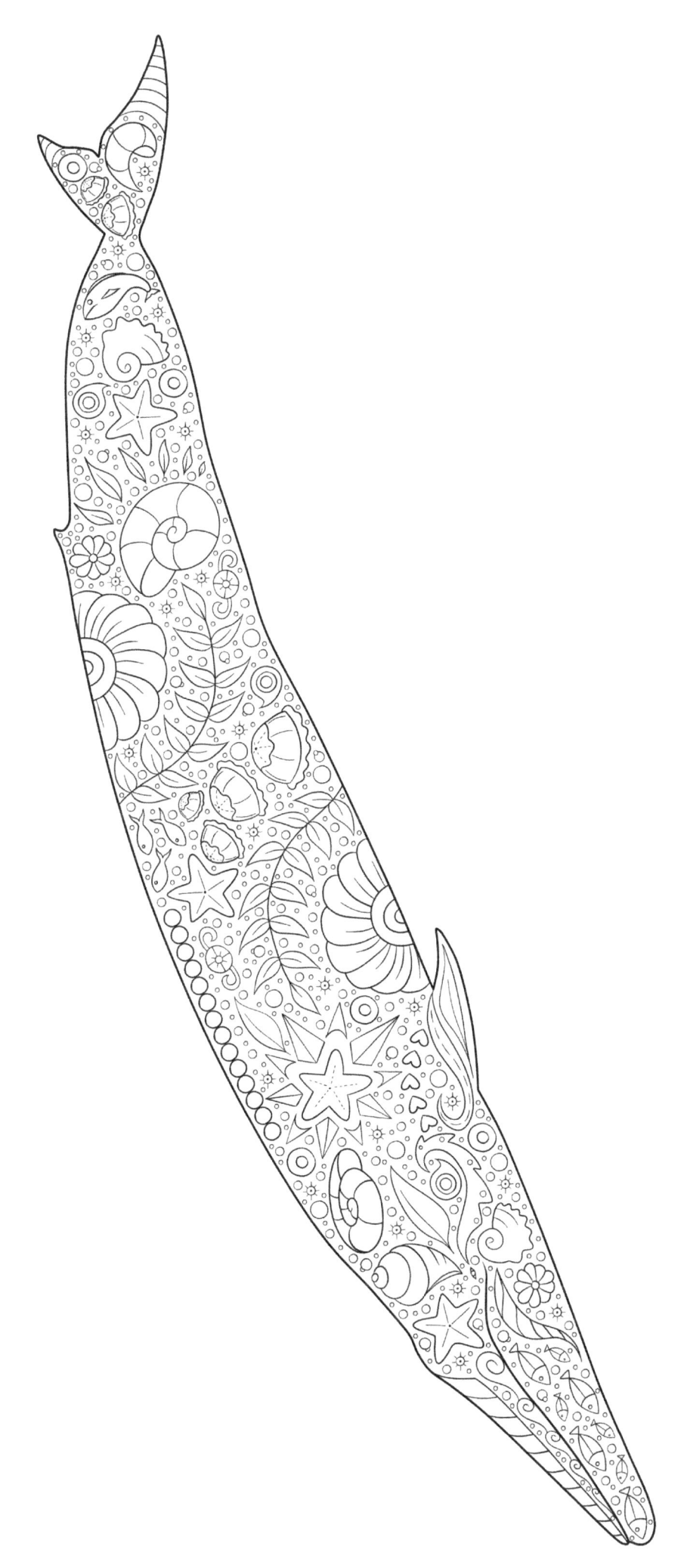

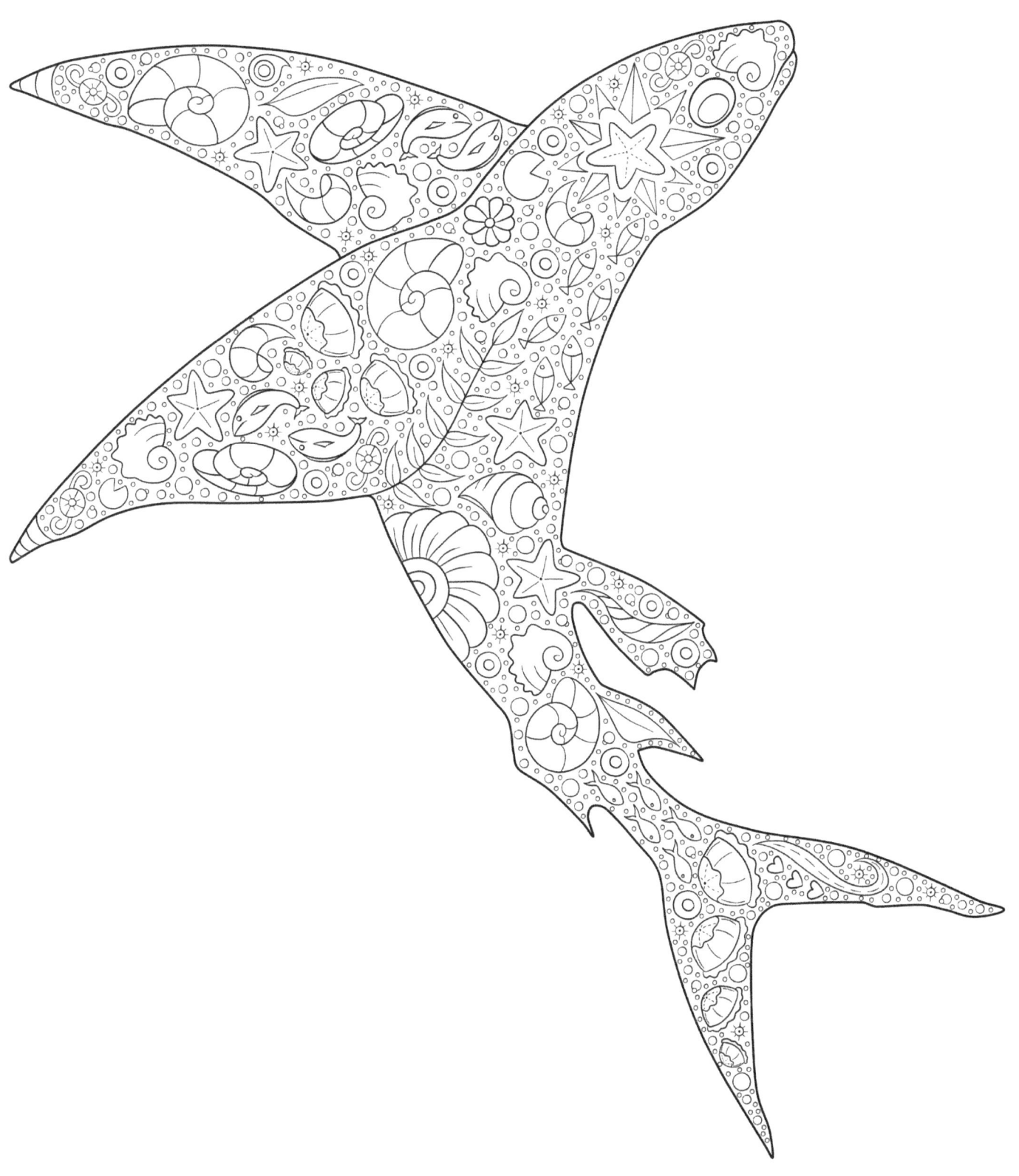

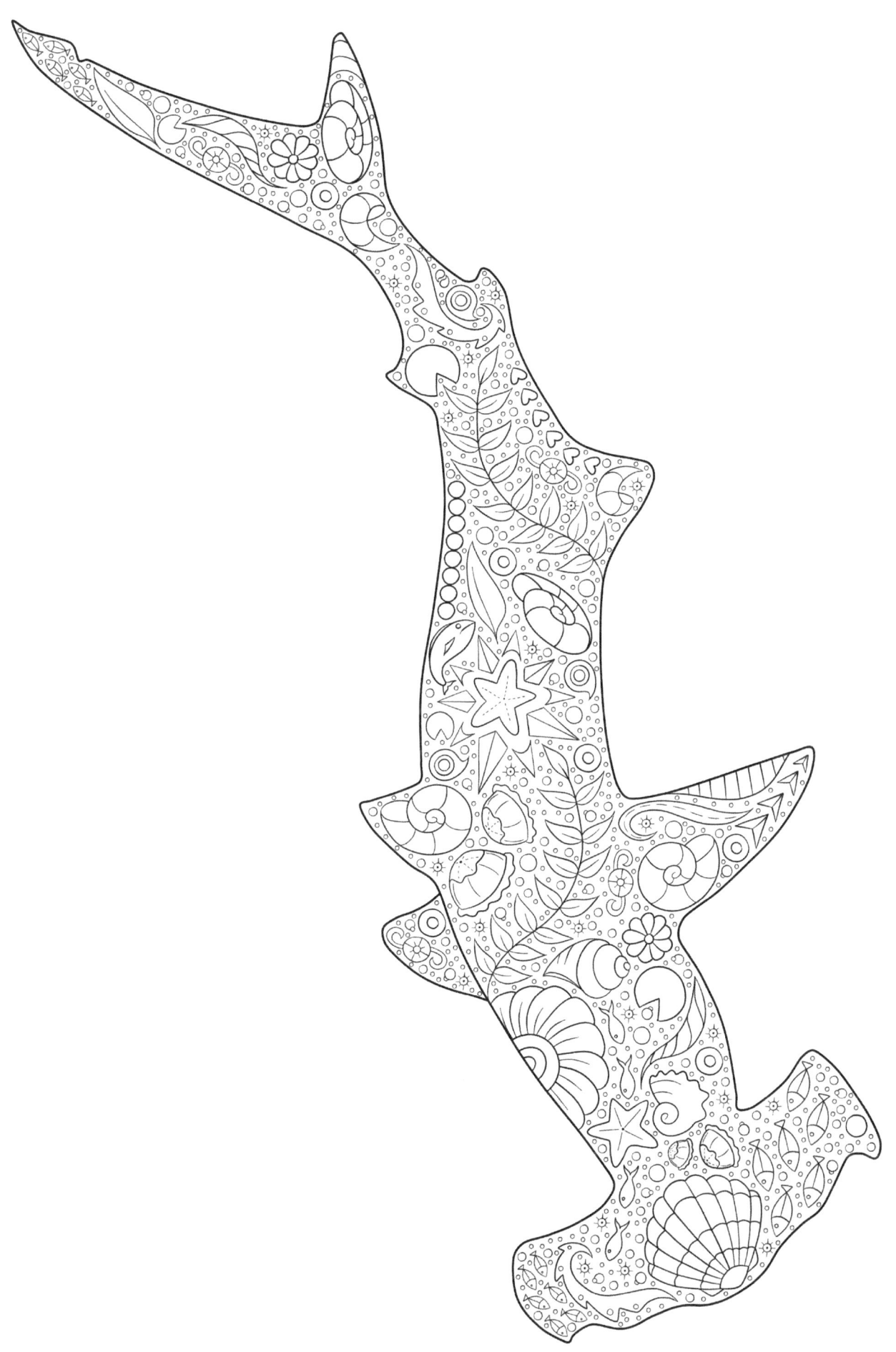

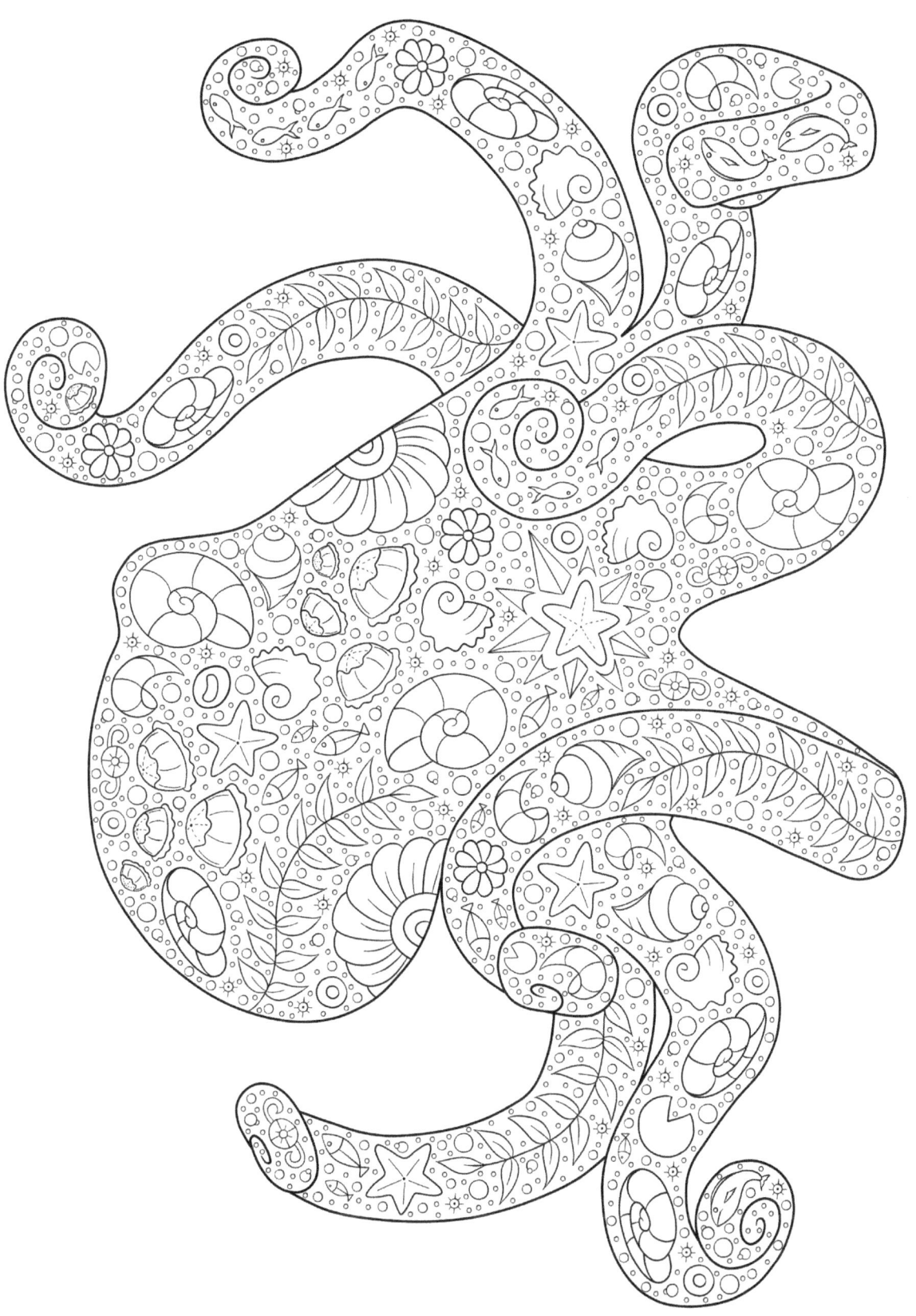

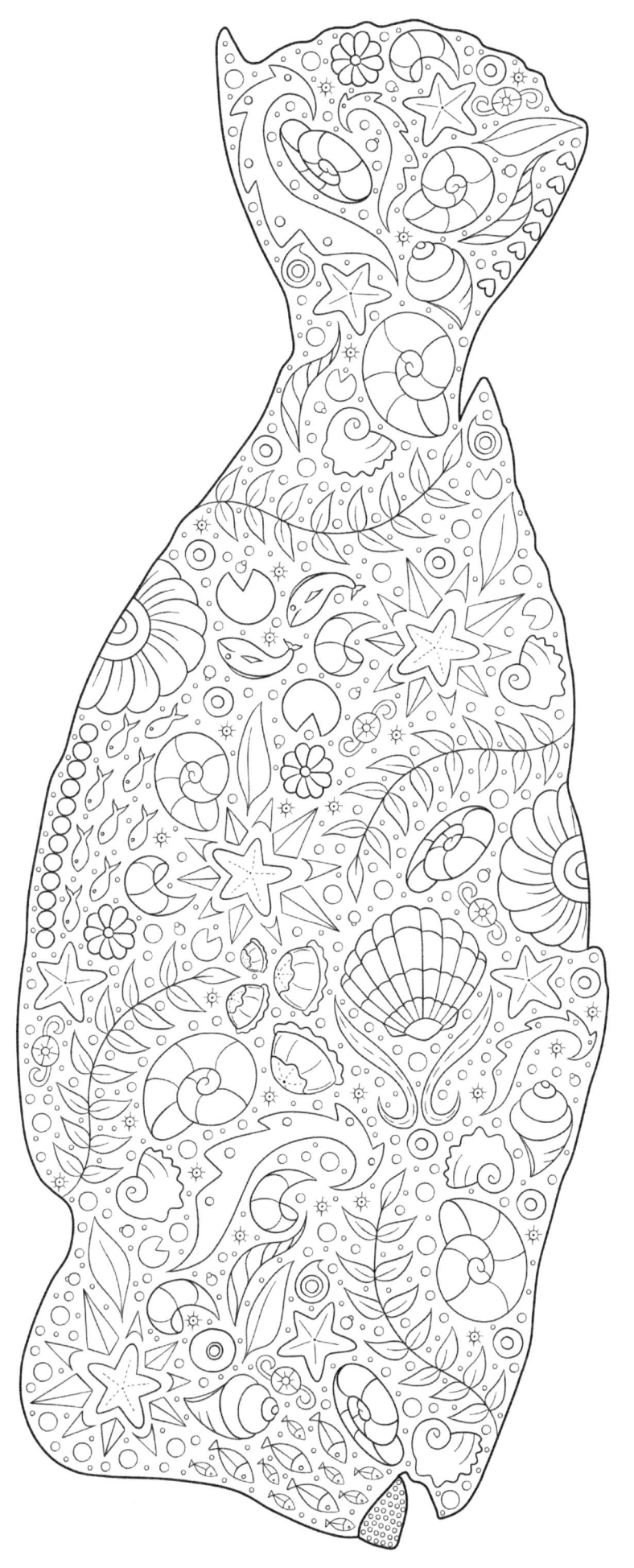

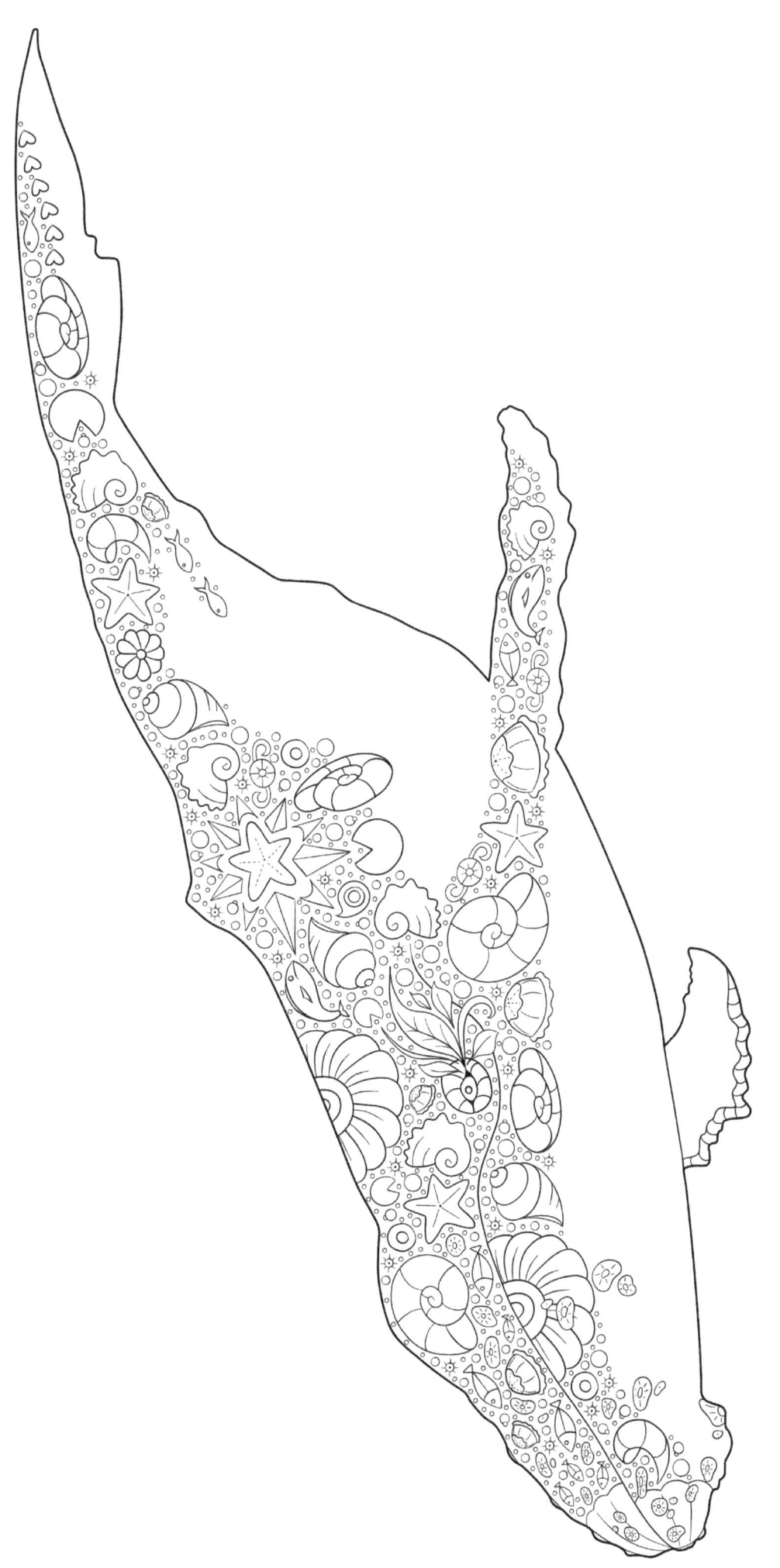

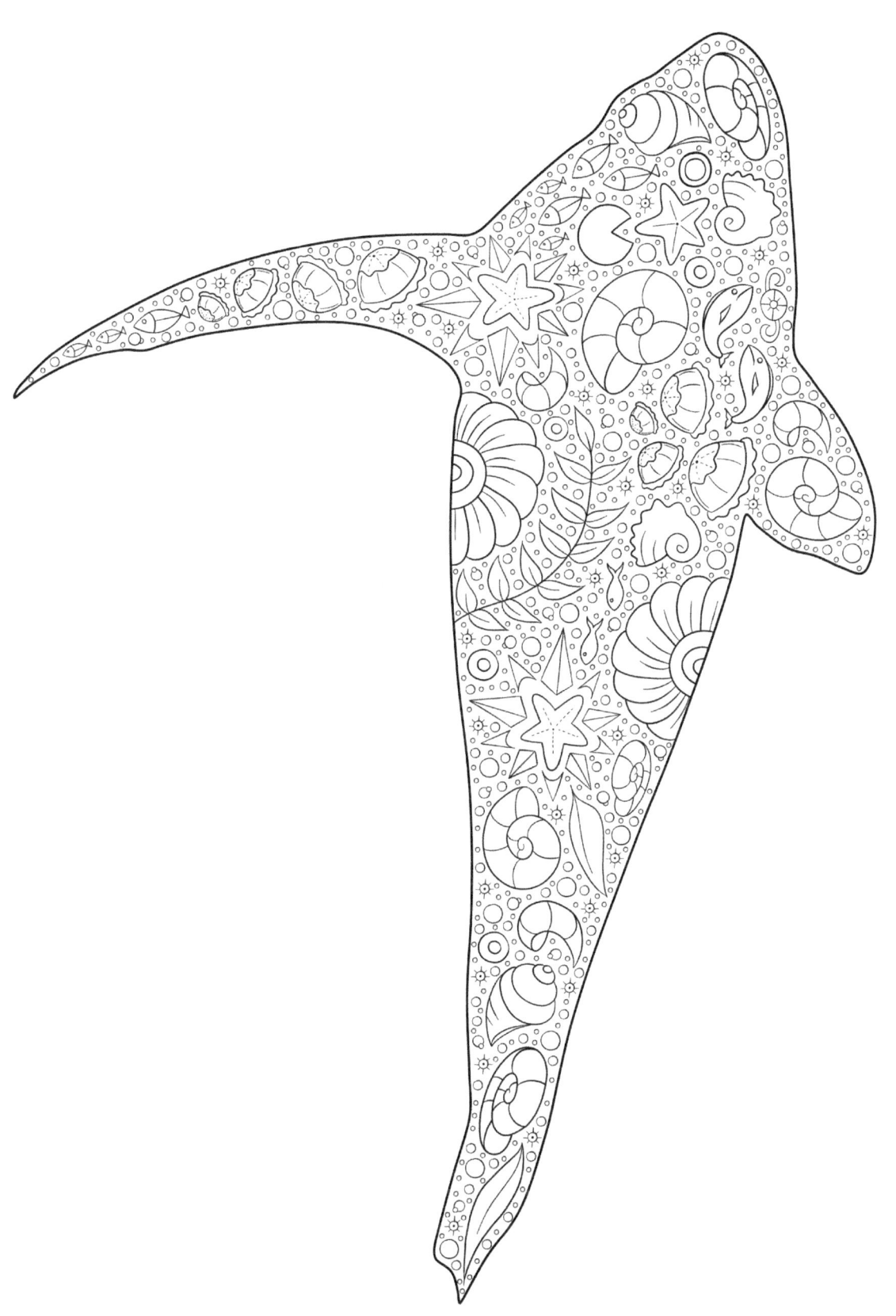

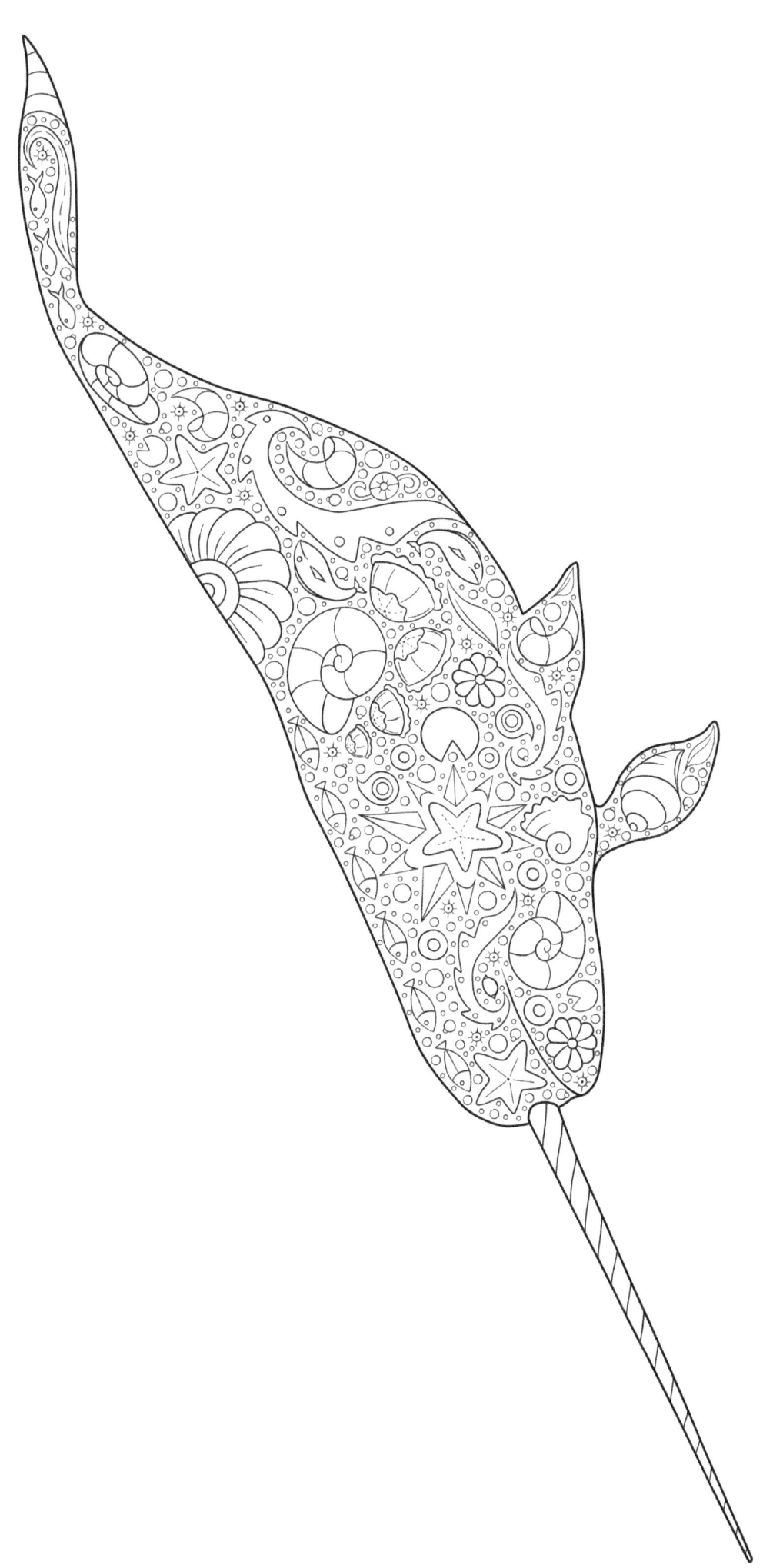

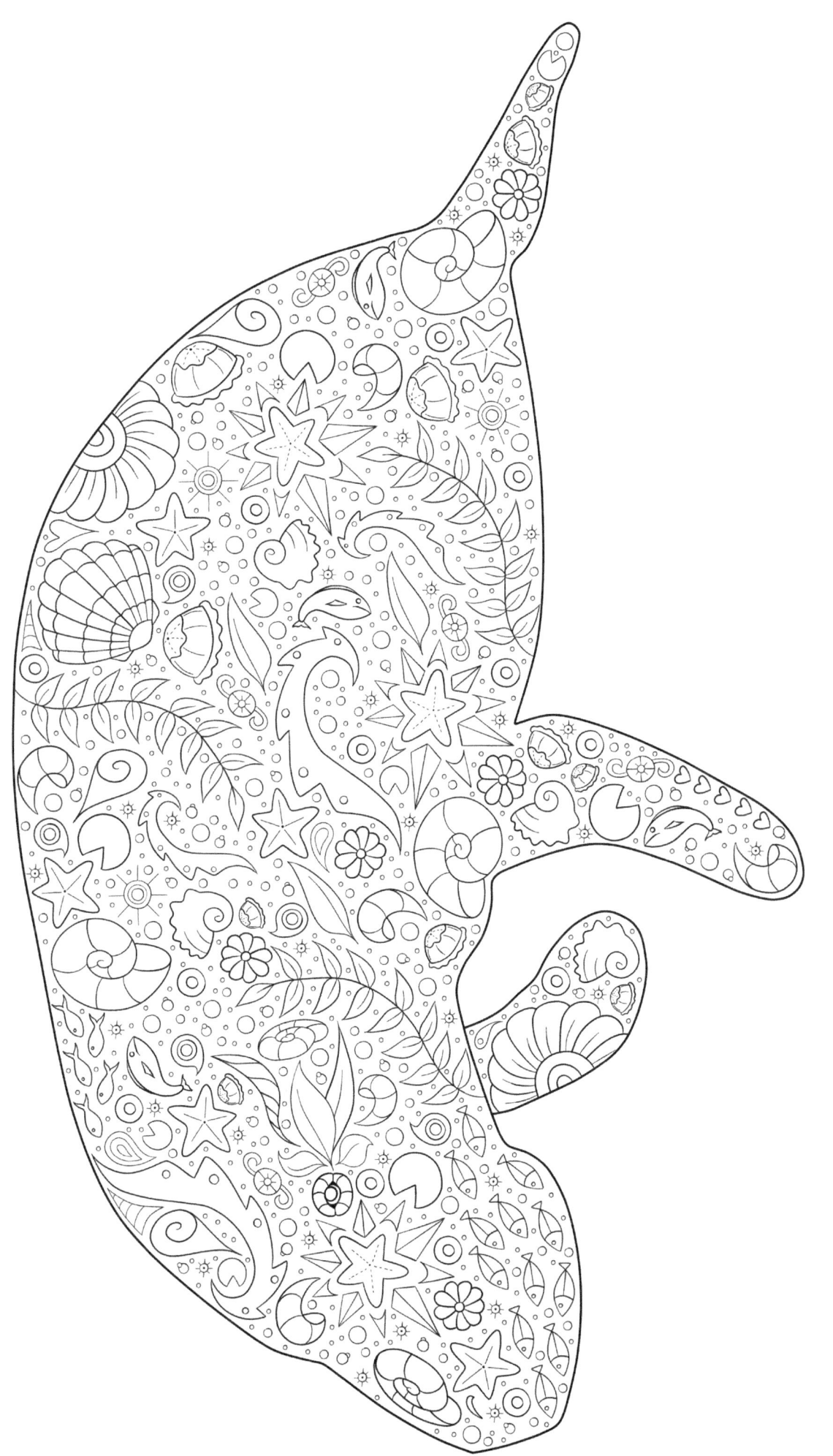

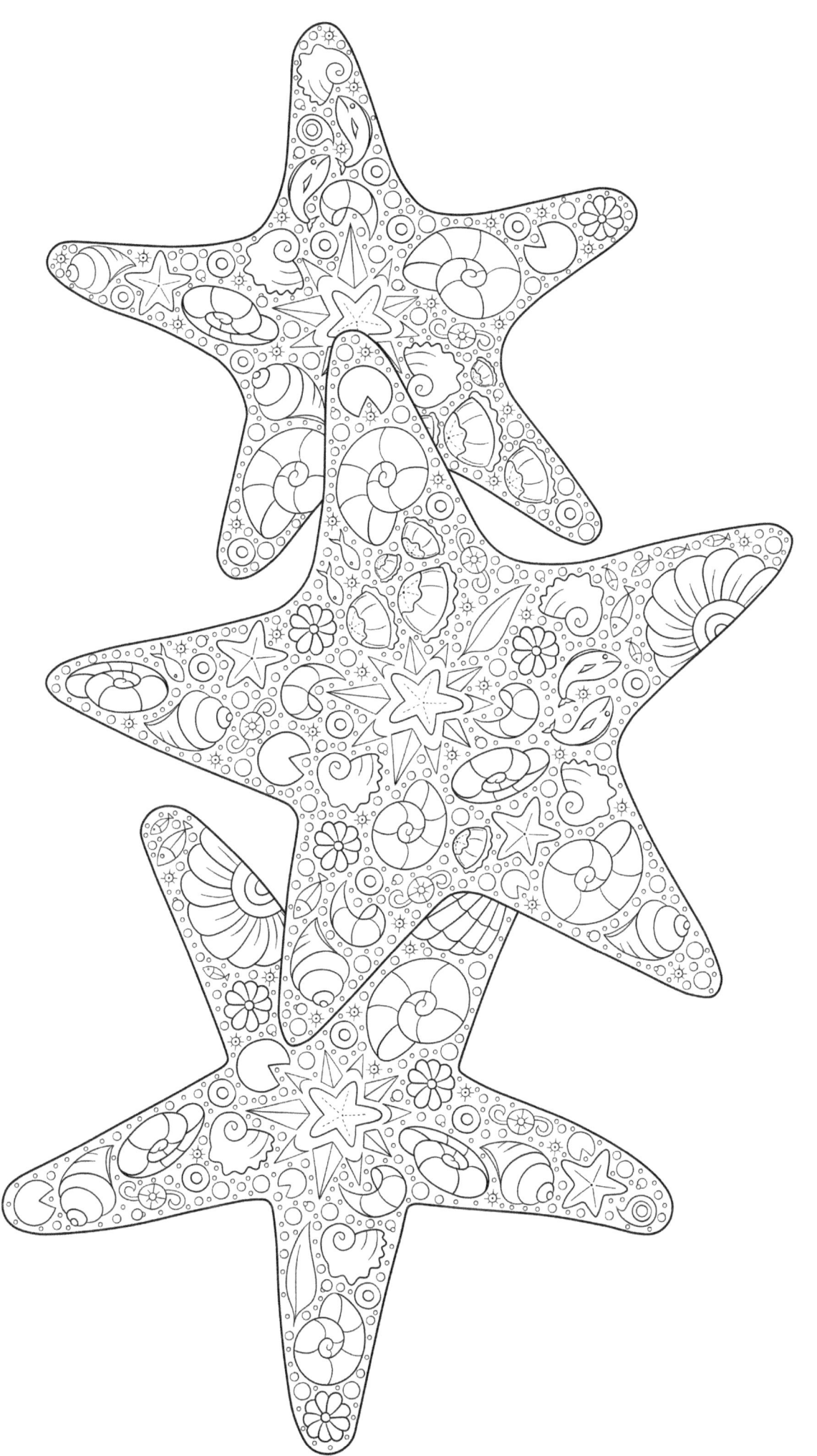

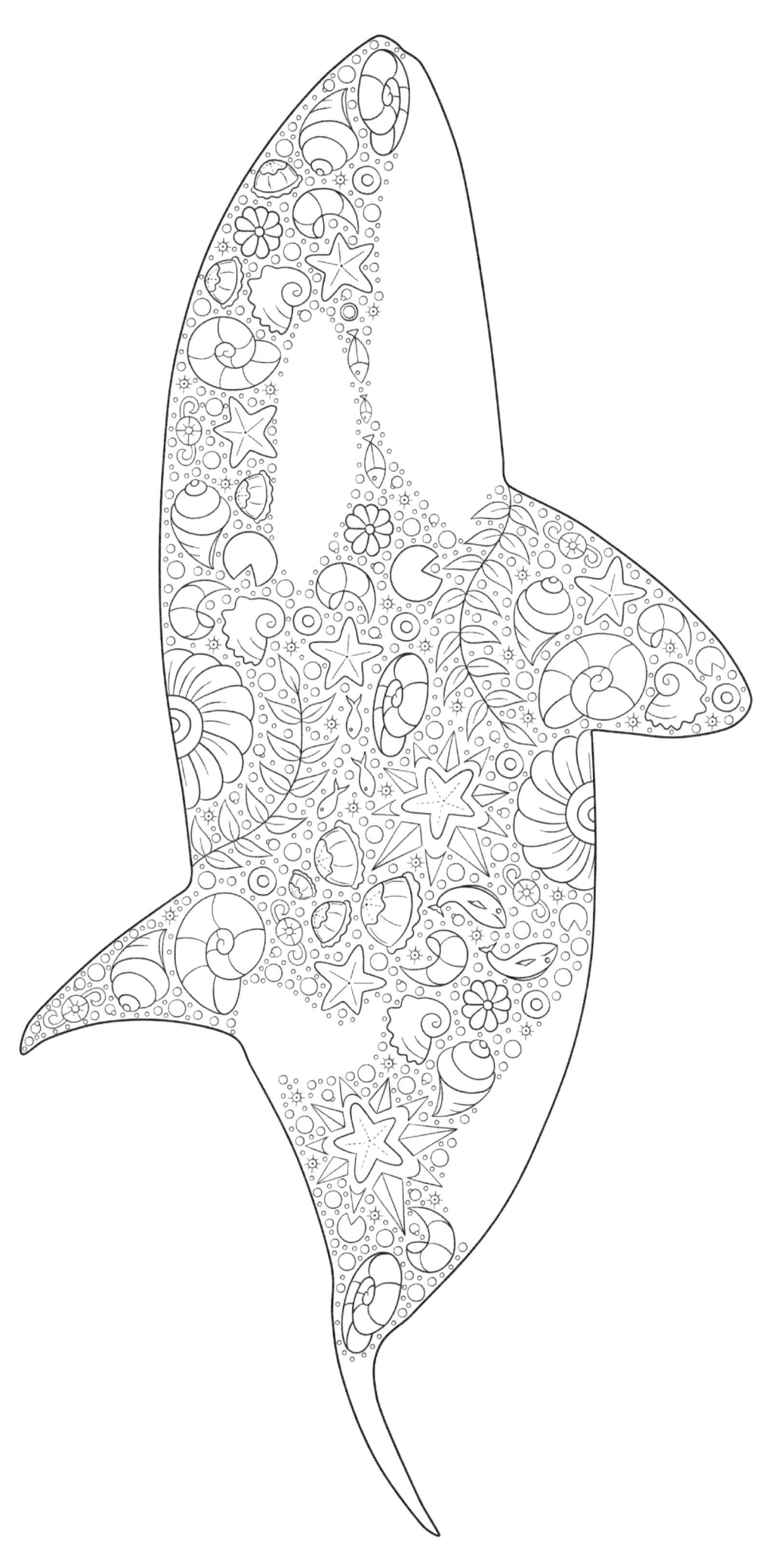

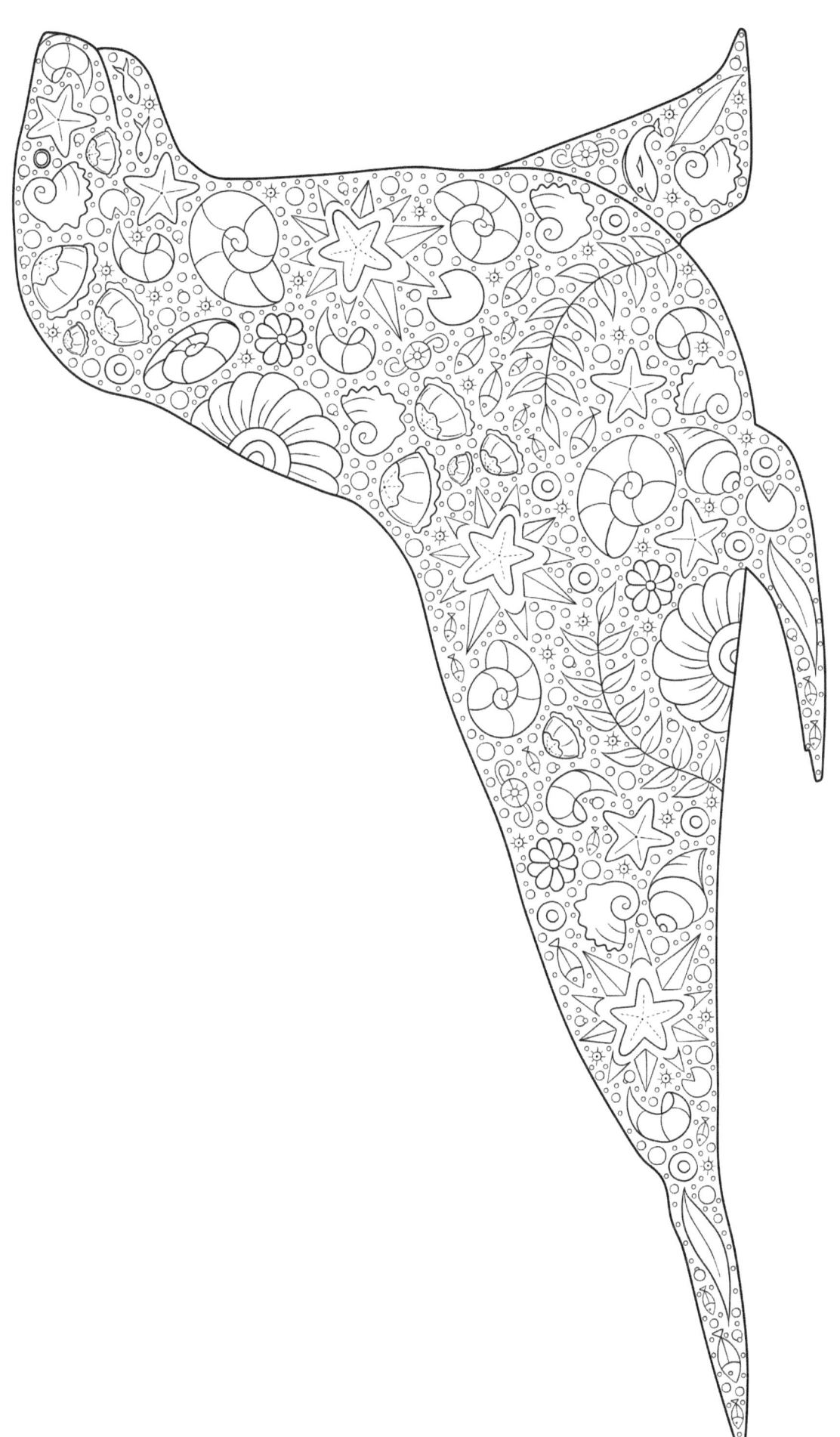

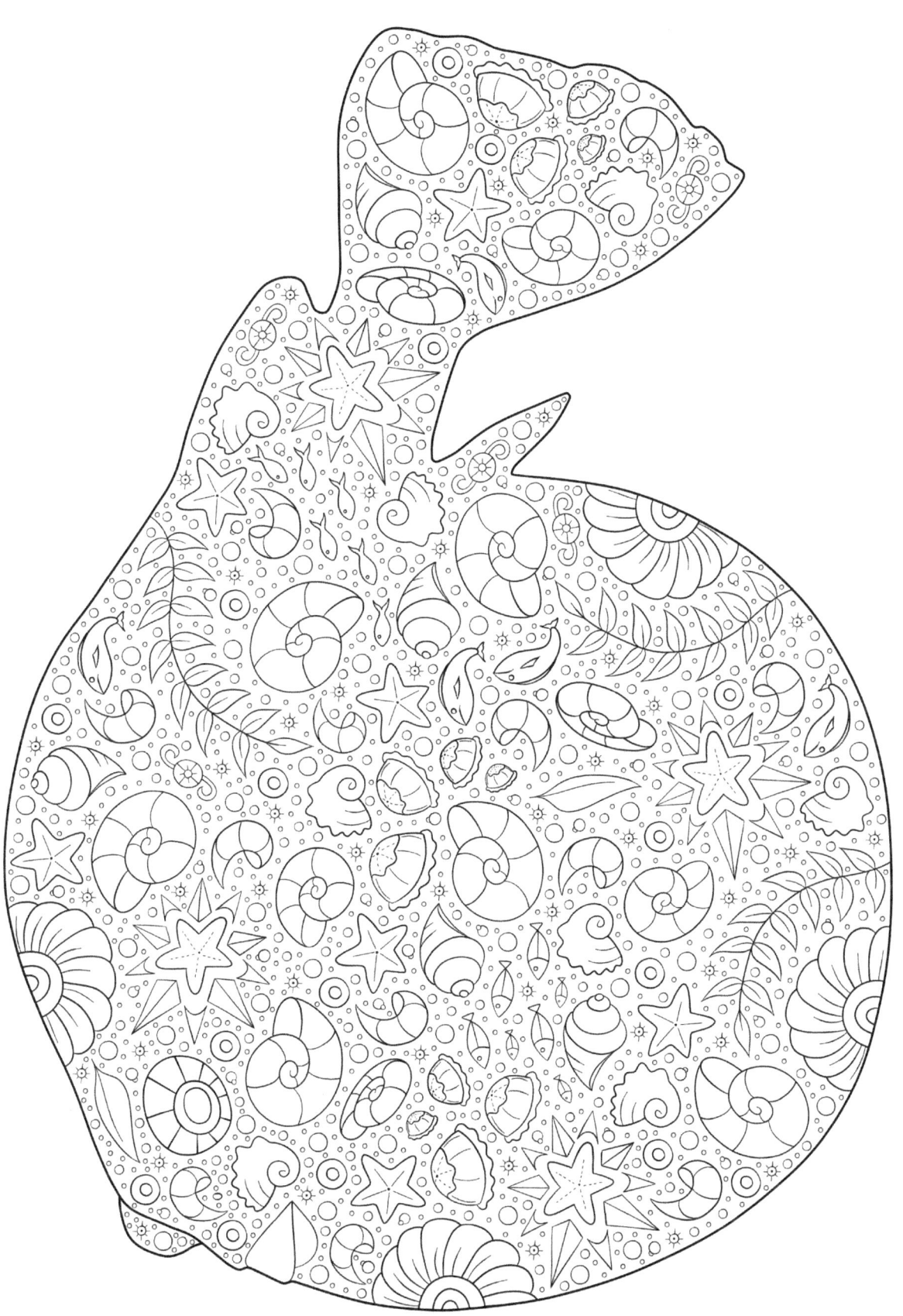

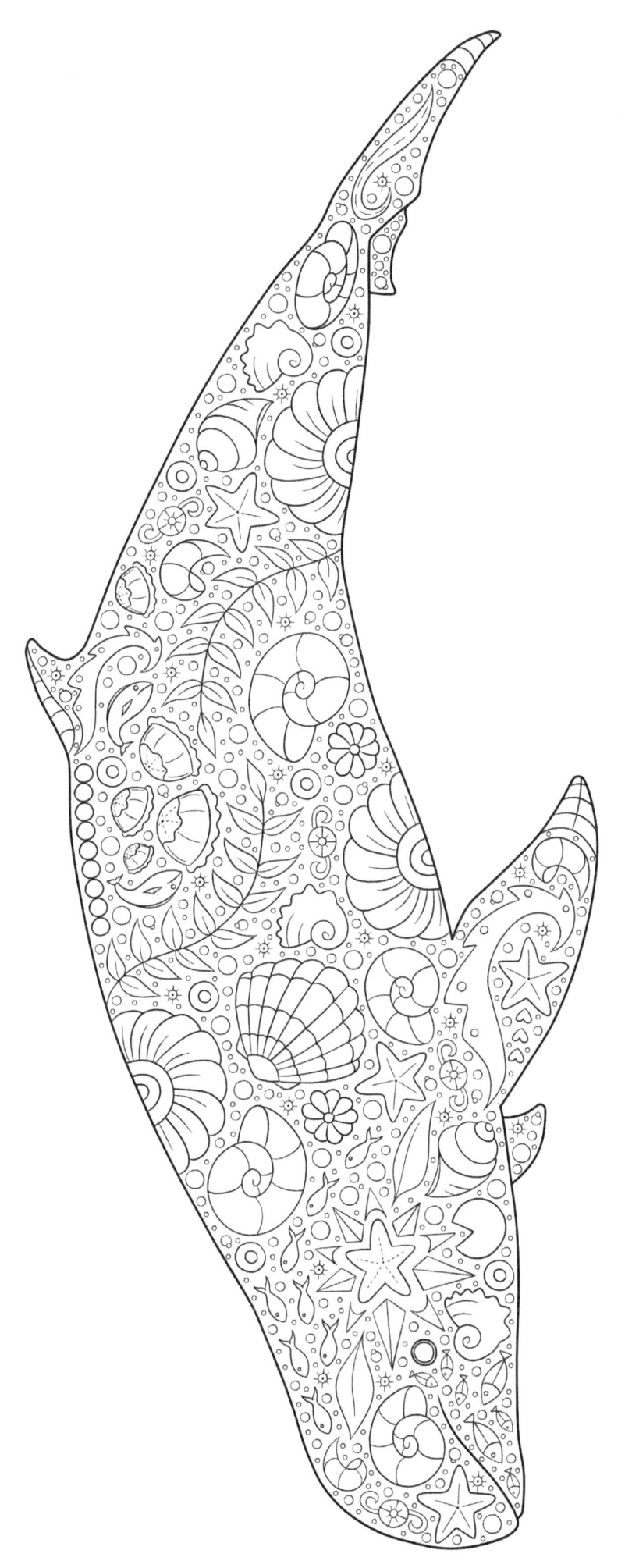

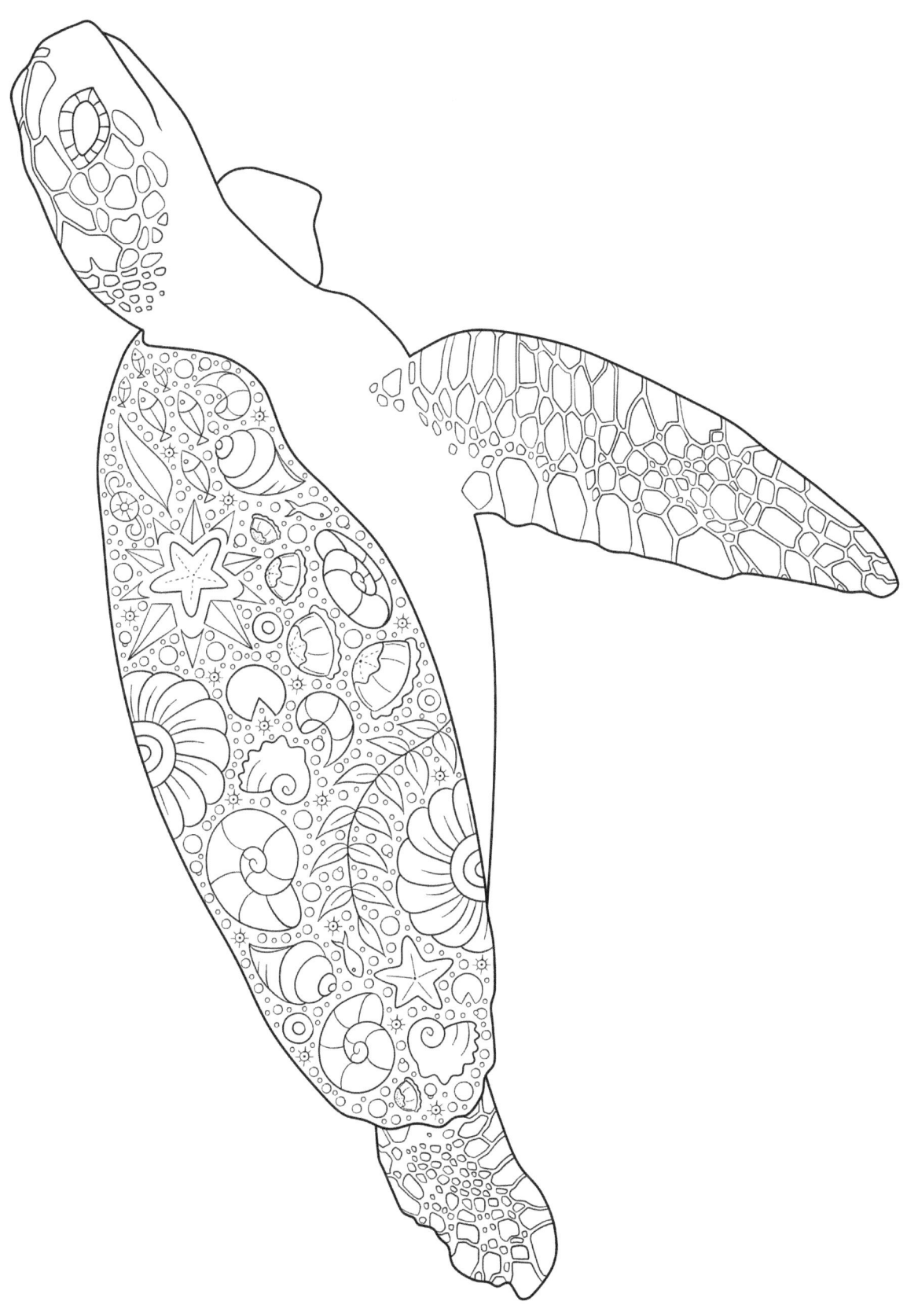

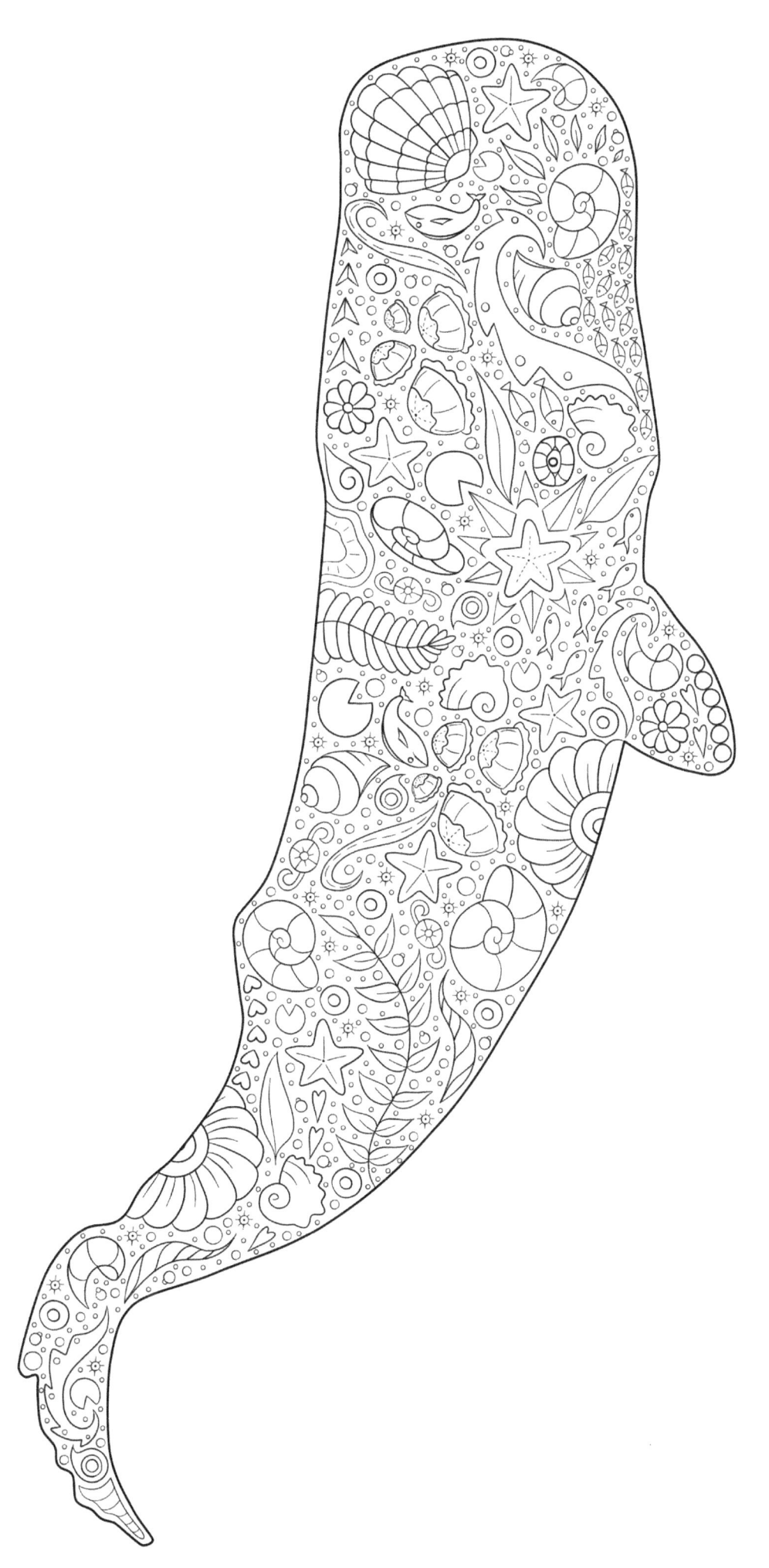

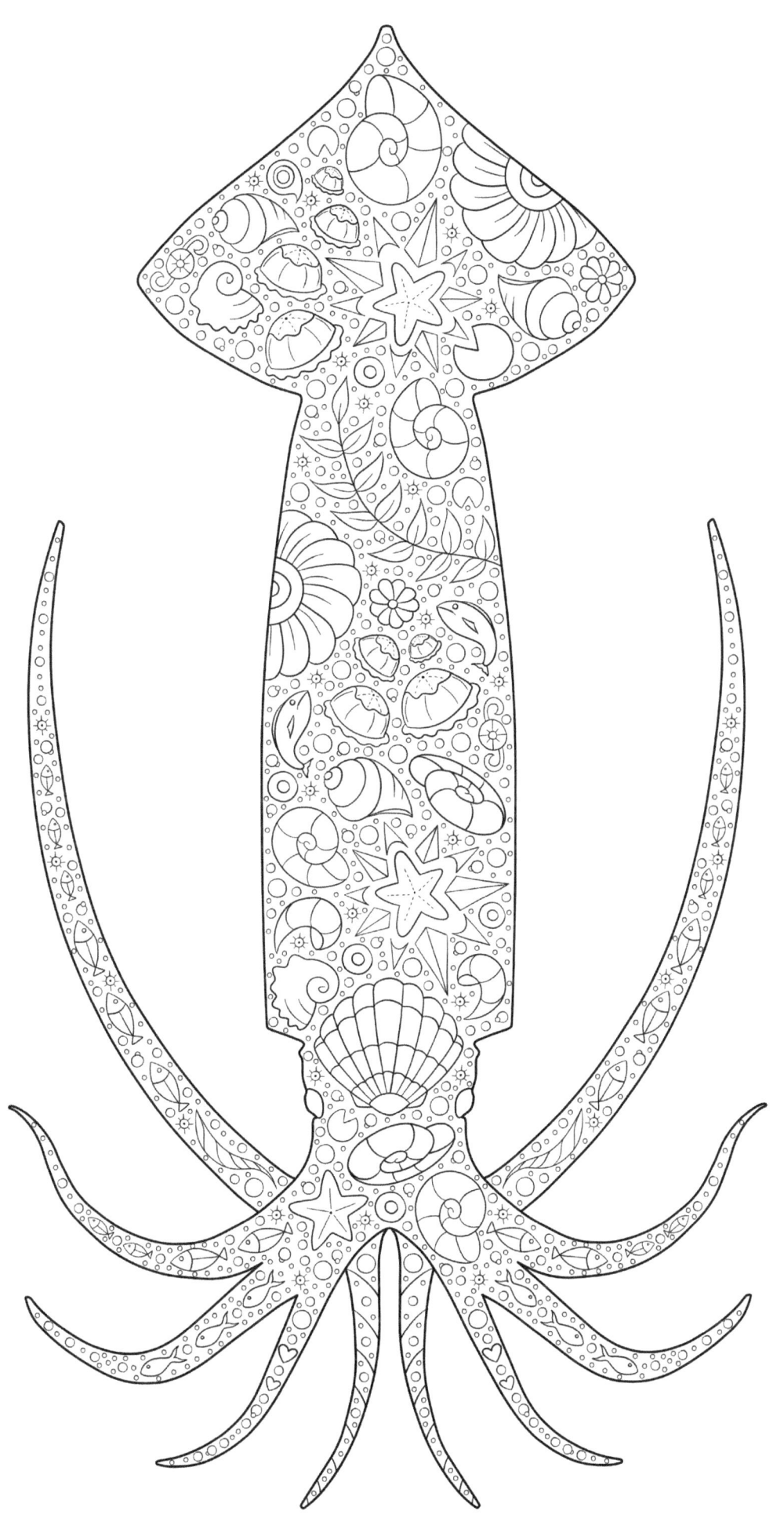

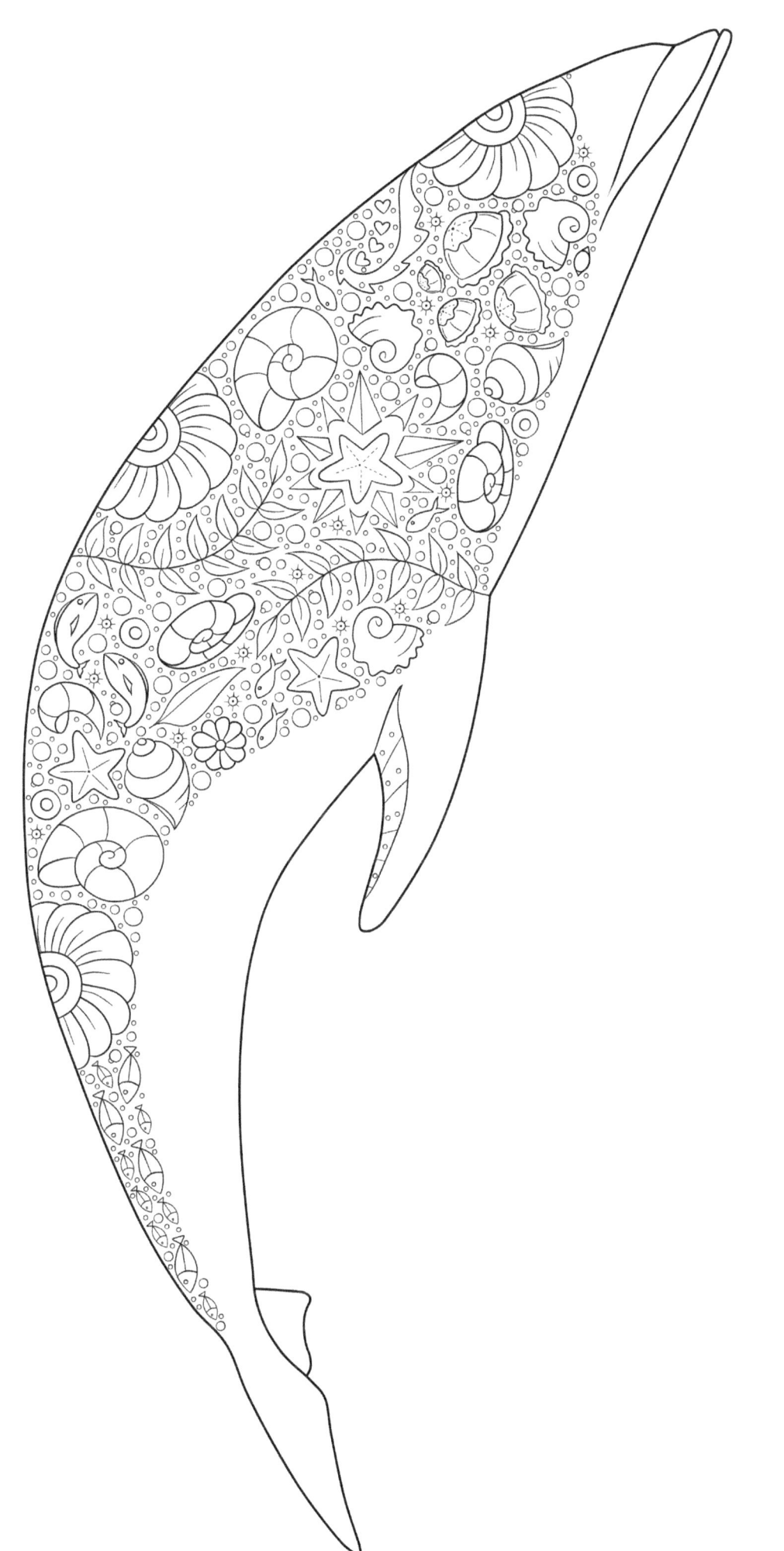

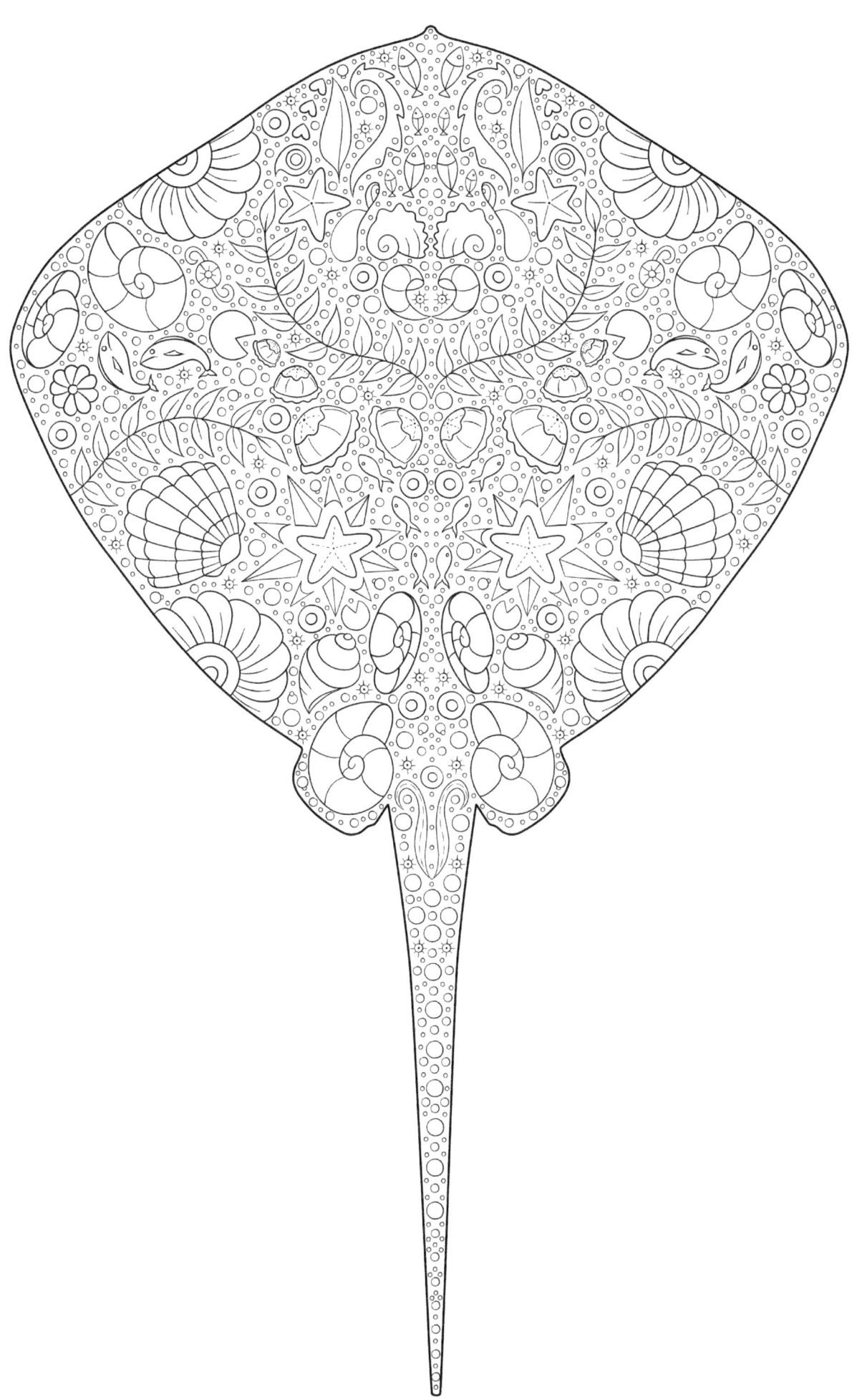

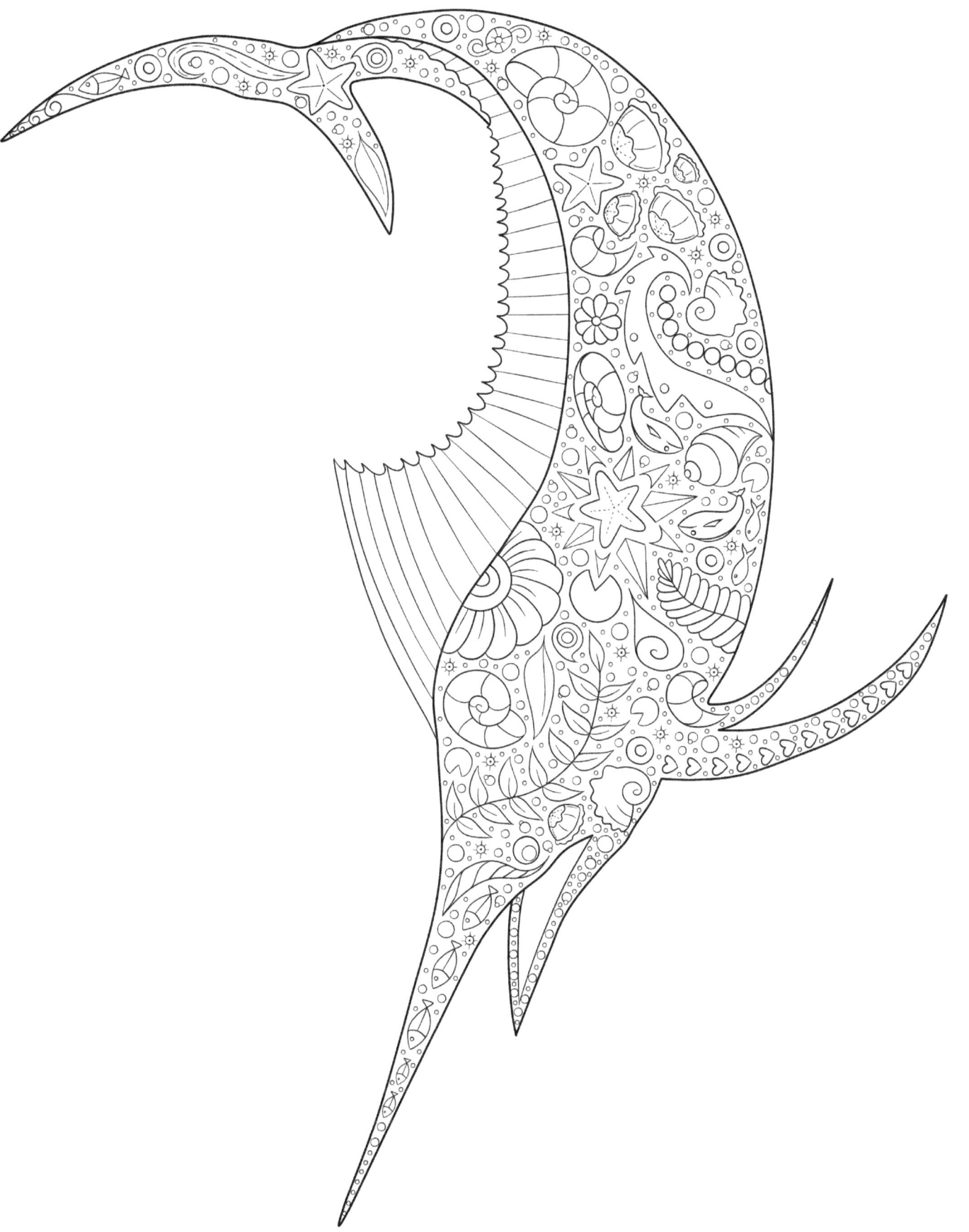

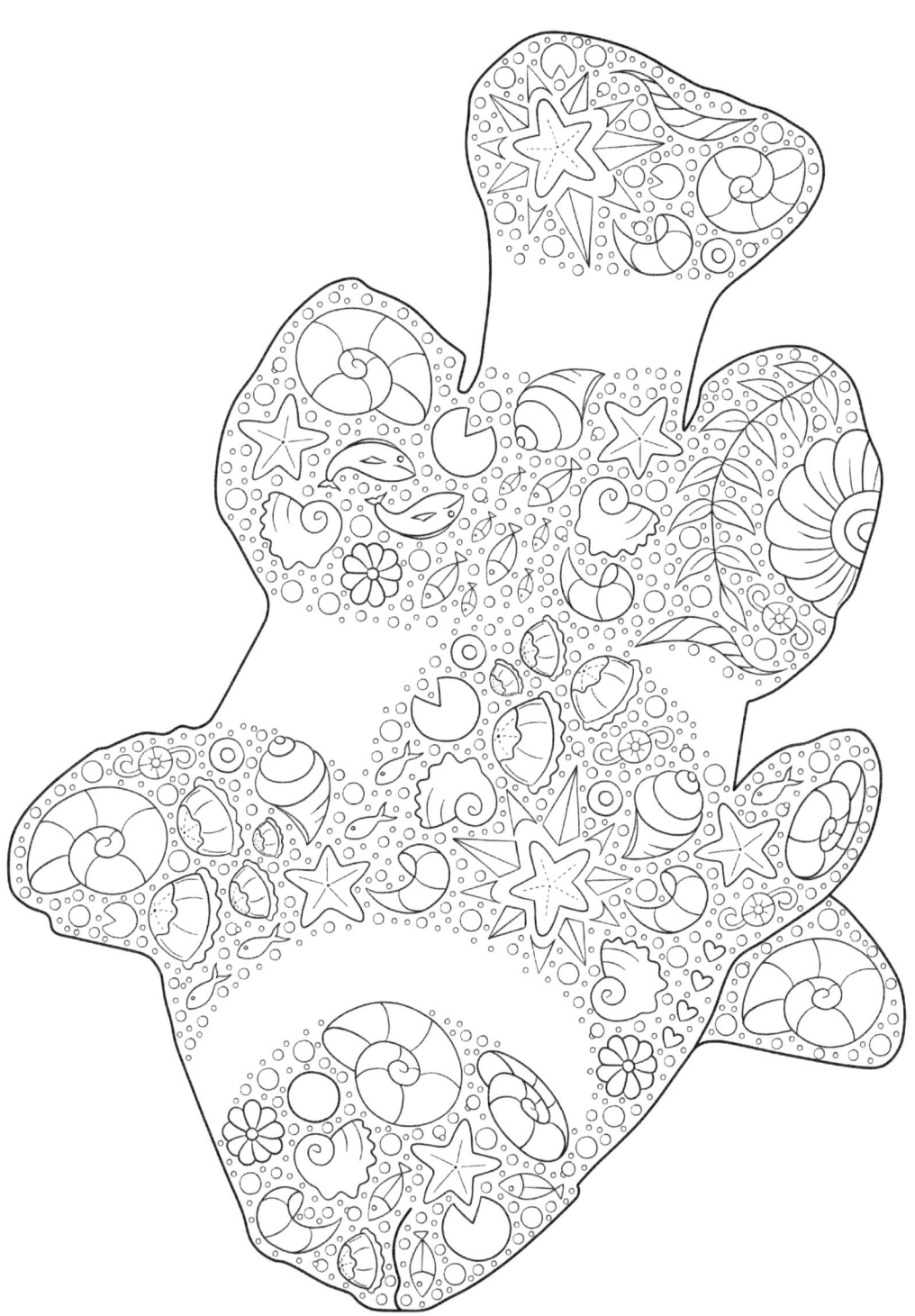

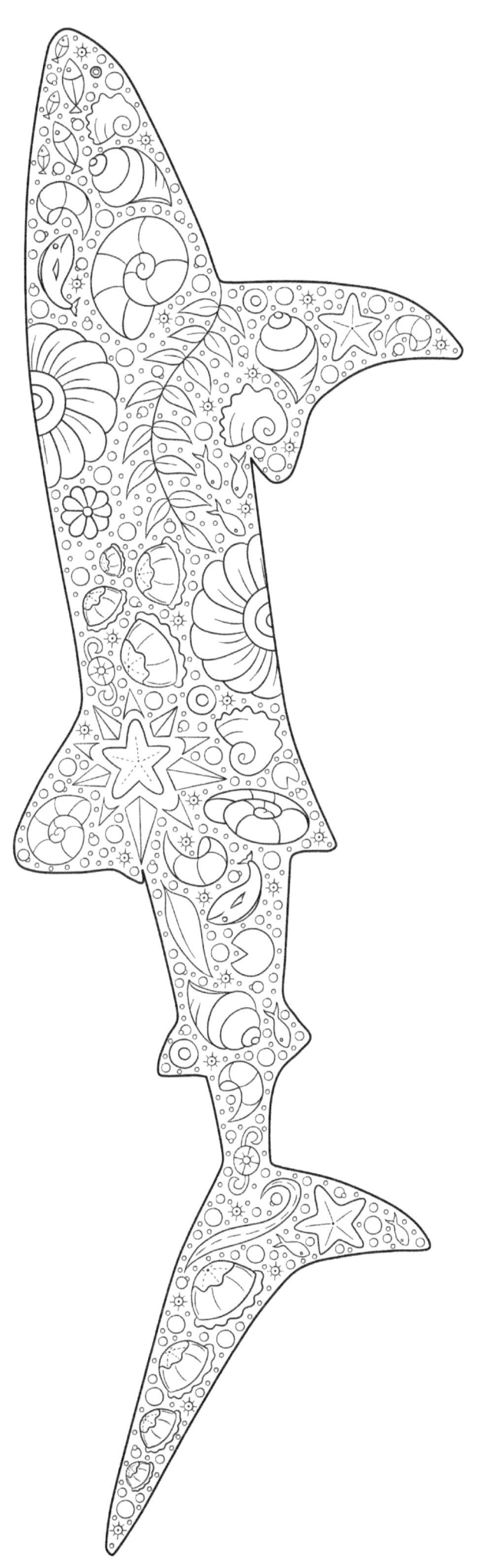

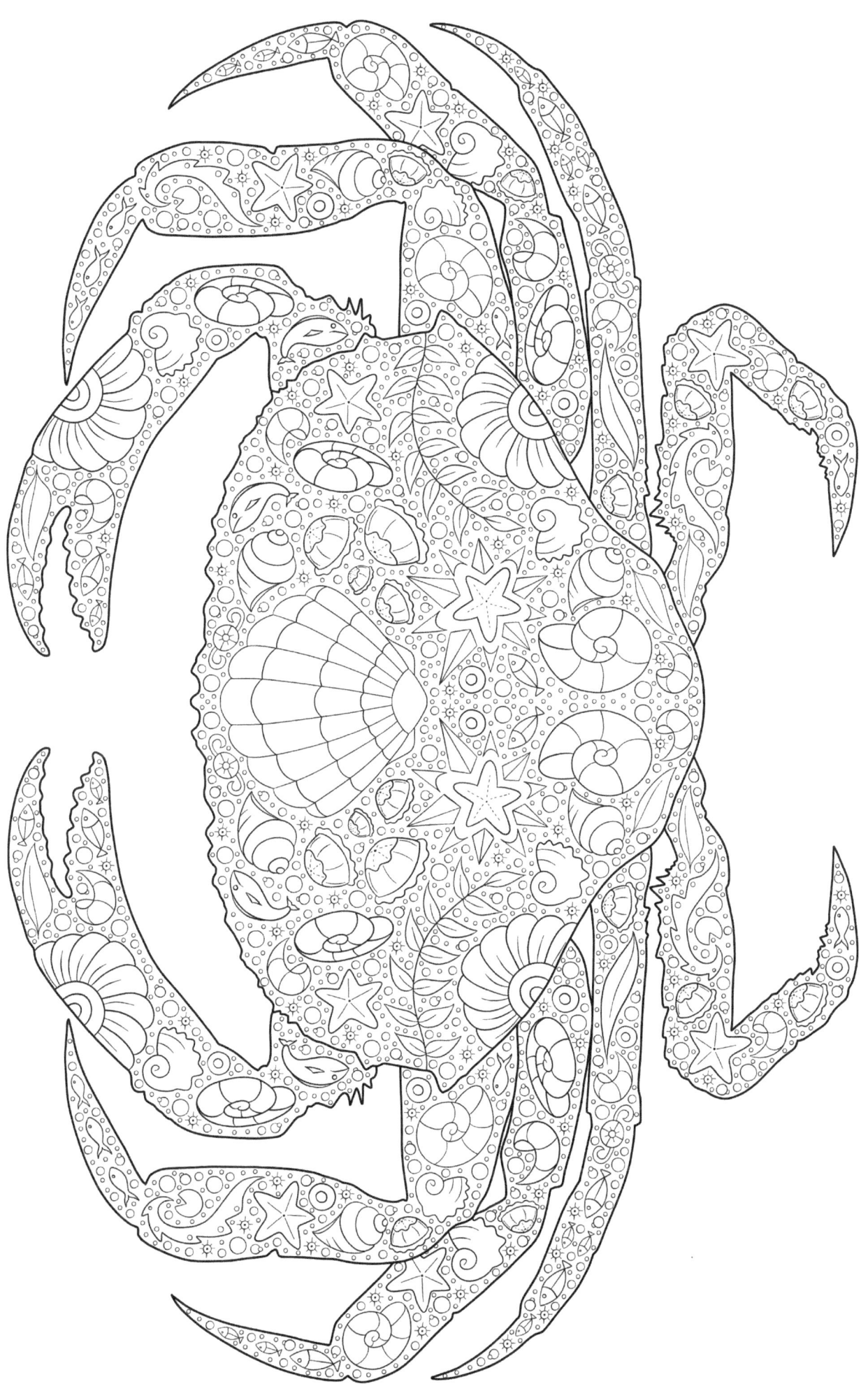